HOW DID WE FIND OUT ABOUT
NUCLEAR POWER?

The "HOW DID WE FIND OUT . . . ?" SERIES
by Isaac Asimov

HOW DID WE FIND OUT—

HOW DID WE FIND OUT

ABOUT NUCLEAR POWER?

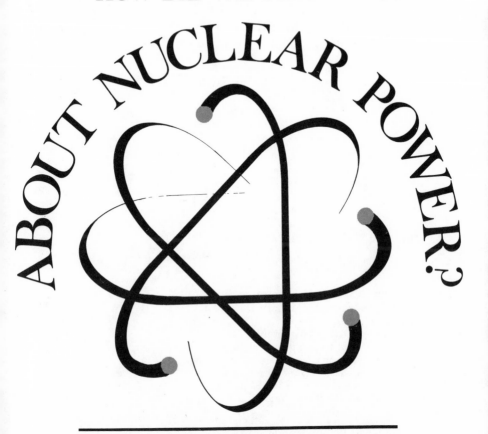

Isaac Asimov
Illustrated by David Wool

WALKER AND COMPANY
New York

To Eleanor Sullivan and Constance DiRienzo,
and their unfailing good nature

THE ASIMOV SCIENCE LIBRARY

Text Copyright © 1976 by Isaac Asimov
Illustrations Copyright © 1976 by David Wool

All rights reserved. No part of this book may
be reproduced or transmitted in any form or by
any means, electronic or mechanical, including
photocopying, recording, or by any information
storage and retrieval system, without permission
in writing from the Publisher.

First published in the United States of America
in 1976 by the Walker Publishing Company, Inc.

Published simultaneously in Canada by Fitzhenry &
Whiteside, Limited, Toronto.

TRADE ISBN: 0-8027-6265-4

REINF. ISBN: 0-8027-6266-2

Library of Congress Catalog Card Number: 76-12057

This edition printed in 1986.

Printed in the United States of America.

10 9 8 7 6

Contents

1 Electrons

THROUGH MOST of the 1800's, scientists thought that the smallest bit of matter was an "atom." Each atom was far too small to be seen even under the best microscopes.

There are over a hundred different kinds of atoms. Each kind, when combined with others of the same kind, makes up an "element" (EL-eh-ment). Iron is made up of iron atoms, sulfur is made up of sulfur atoms, oxygen (OK-sih-jen) is made up of oxygen atoms, and so on. Iron, sulfur, and oxygen are examples of elements.

One thing that doesn't seem to be matter is electricity. Electricity is something that flows through various solids and liquids. It travels along wires and can make them glow; it makes motors turn, and so on. Scientists wondered what electricity was made of, since it didn't seem to be made of atoms.

If electricity could be taken out of the wires it flowed through, it might be more easily studied. An electric current can sometimes be made to flash through the air as a bright spark. Such sparks don't last long, however, and are hard to study. Besides, the electric spark is mixed with the various atoms making up the air and that confuses things.

Suppose an electric current is made to pass through a vacuum (VAK-yoo-um), that is, through space that contains nothing at all, not even air.

For this to be possible, a tube must have all the air pumped out of it. There must also be two metal plates in different places, inside the tube, so that the electric current can be forced from one plate to the other.

Back in 1855, over a hundred years ago, a German inventor, Heinrich Geissler (GISE-ler), was the first to construct such vacuum tubes. Scientists were then able to study electric currents forced through a vacuum. They found that something was produced that travelled in straight lines and could therefore be called "radiation" (RAY-dee-AY-shun) or "rays."

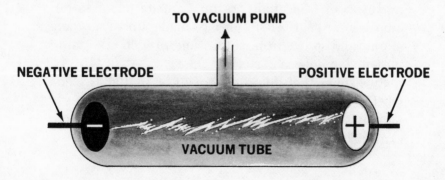

TO VACUUM PUMP

NEGATIVE ELECTRODE   POSITIVE ELECTRODE

VACUUM TUBE

They could tell the radiation was there because it glowed faintly. Where it hit the glass of the tube, the glass glowed more strongly.

In 1876, a German scientist, Eugen Goldstein, showed that the radiation started at the plate called a "cathode" (KATH-ode). He called the radiation "cathode rays" for that reason.

Some people thought that the cathode rays were a kind of light. Light is made up of tiny waves of a certain length. Perhaps cathode rays were made up of tiny waves of the same kind but of a slightly different length.

If a magnet were brought near the vacuum tube, however, the path of the cathode rays curved. That was not how light behaved. Light travelled in a straight line whether a magnet was present or not.

A French scientist, Jean Baptiste Perrin (peh-RAN) showed, in 1895, that the cathode rays carried an electric charge. That was why the path curved—a magnet can pull at an electric charge.

Bits of matter can carry an electric charge, but light can't. Perrin decided, therefore, that cathode rays were made up of tiny electrically charged particles.

In 1897, an English scientist, Joseph John Thomson, studied that curved path of the cathode rays. From the strength of the magnetic pull, and from the amount of curve in the path, he could calculate the actual size of the little particles. He discovered, to his surprise, that the cathode ray particles were far smaller than atoms. A cathode ray particle was only 1/1800 the size of even the smallest atom!

JOSEPH JOHN THOMSON

Because the cathode ray particles were smaller than atoms, they were "subatomic particles," the first ever to be discovered. Thomson called them "electrons" because they were found in an electric current.

Scientists now knew two different classes of particles. There were the tiny atoms which made up matter, and the even tinier electrons which made up electricity. Was there a connection between the two?

The answer to that arose out of other experiments in connection with cathode rays. In 1895, a German scientist, Wilhelm Konrad Roentgen (ROINT-gen) found that when cathode rays struck matter, a new kind of radiation was formed. This new radiation could make certain chemicals glow and could darken a photographic plate. It could do so even when the chemicals or the plate were hidden behind a piece of cardboard or wood. The radiation could pass right through solid matter.

Roentgen didn't know what the radiation was so he called it "X-rays." "X" is the usual mathematical symbol for something that is unknown. Eventually it turned out that X-rays were made up of waves similar to light waves, but much shorter.

Once Roentgen announced his discovery, other scientists began to try to find X-rays elsewhere.

A French scientist, Antoine Henri Becquerel (beh-KREL) was working with a chemical compound containing atoms of an element named uranium (yoo-RAY-nee-um). The compound glowed when sunlight fell on it, and Becquerel wondered if the glow contained X-rays.

WILHELM KONRAD ROENTGEN

Becquerel exposed the compound to the sun. He then wrapped it in black paper and placed it near a photographic plate in the dark. If the glow were ordinary light, it would not pass through the black paper, and the photographic plate would be unchanged. If the glow contained X-rays, those would pass through the paper and, when the plate was developed, it would prove to be darkened.

The plate was darkened, and Becquerel thought he had X-rays in the glow. He wanted to try again,

BECQUEREL'S EXPERIMENT

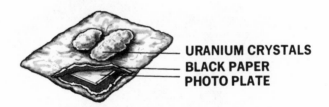

URANIUM CRYSTALS
BLACK PAPER
PHOTO PLATE

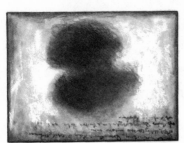

**PHOTOGRAPHIC PLATE
SHOWS RADIOACTIVITY**

MARIE CURIE

though, to make sure. However, the next day was cloudy, and the skies stayed cloudy for several days. Becquerel had the compound wrapped in black paper near another plate and just waited for the sun.

Finally, bored with waiting, he developed the photographic plate just to see if the glow from that one day of sun was still hanging on just a little. He found the plate had darkened a great deal. The compound was giving off radiations even *without* being exposed to the sun. In fact, further experiments showed that the compound gave off radiation all the time.

A Polish-French scientist, Marie Sklowdowska Curie (kyoo-REE), showed in 1898 that it was the uranium atom in the compound that was actively giving off the radiation. Curie called uranium a radioactive (RAY-dee-oh-AK-tiv) substance. She also showed that the atoms of another element, thorium (THAW-ree-um), were radioactive.

It turned out that uranium and thorium gave off three kinds of radiation. Some of the radiation curved slightly in one direction in the presence of a magnet. Another part of the radiation curved in the other direction, and by a much greater amount. Still another part of the radiation just moved straight on as though the magnet weren't there.

A New Zealand scientist, Ernest Rutherford, named the three radiations after the first three letters of the Greek alphabet. The radiations that curved slightly were named "alpha rays" (AL-fuh) after the first letter. Those that curved quite a bit were "beta rays" (BAY-tuh) after the second letter. Those that didn't curve at all were "gamma rays" (GAM-uh) after the third letter.

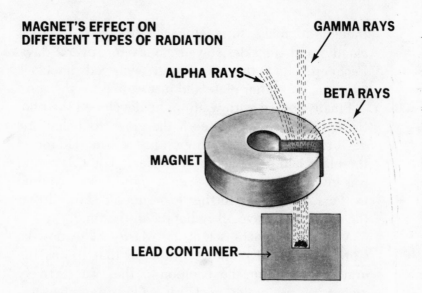

MAGNET'S EFFECT ON DIFFERENT TYPES OF RADIATION

GAMMA RAYS

ALPHA RAYS

BETA RAYS

MAGNET

LEAD CONTAINER →

Because the gamma rays didn't curve, it seemed likely that they resembled light and X-rays. That turned out to be so. Gamma rays are made up of waves that are even shorter than those of X-rays.

As for the beta rays, the fact that they curved when near a magnet meant that they must be made up of electrically charged "beta particles." The path curved so much that the beta particles had to be very light in weight. In 1900, Becquerel was able to show that beta particles were indeed light in weight, since they were electrons.

That was a puzzler, in a way. When electrons were discovered, they seemed to be particles of an electric current. Now they seemed to be coming out of uranium and thorium atoms. Yet there was no electric current in these atoms. What were the electrons doing there?

At that time, uranium and thorium were the substances with the heaviest known atoms. Perhaps there was something about very heavy atoms that made them special, and different from the rest.

It turned out, though, that they weren't so different.

In 1899, Thomson was working with ultra-violet light, which is made up of waves just a little shorter than the waves of ordinary light. Thomson studied what happened when the ultra-violet light shone on the surfaces of certain metallic elements.

The shorter the waves of any variety of light, the more energy that variety has. The short ultra-violet waves struck the metal surface harder than the longer waves of ordinary light did.

When ordinary light shines on a metal surface, nothing usually happens. The ultra-violet light, however, struck hard enough to knock something out of the metal. Thomson found that it was electrons that were knocked out of the metal. He called this the "photoelectric effect," since "photo" is from a Greek word meaning "light."

As scientists studied the photoelectric effect, it seemed that electrons could be knocked out of any piece of matter at all, if it were knocked hard enough.

The electrons had to come from the atoms, since every piece of matter is made of atoms and nothing else. That meant that scientists couldn't consider atoms to be little balls with nothing smaller in them. They contained electrons.

In fact, that was how an electric current must start

flowing. Electrons must somehow be pried out of atoms and sent moving through matter. *That was the connection between matter and electricity.*

Thomson was the first to try to figure out what atoms looked like, now that electrons had been discovered. He thought that atoms must be little balls with electrons stuck here and there to the outside, like raisins on a piece of cake.

It was an interesting thought, but it was wrong.

2 Nuclei

ONE TROUBLE with Thomson's idea was that it didn't take the alpha rays into account.

The path of alpha rays curved under the pull of a magnet and this meant they had to be made up of flying, electrically charged particles. The path of these "alpha particles" curved only slightly, however. Could it be that the electric charge on alpha particles was much smaller than on electrons so that the magnet pulled it less forcefully?

No! After careful study, it turned out that an alpha particle had just twice the electric charge that an electron had, and it was an opposite kind of electric charge since the alpha particle curved in the opposite direction from the election. The electric charge on an electron is said to be negative and its size is said to be —1. The electric charge on the alpha particle is positive and, since it is twice as large as that on the electron, it is listed as +2.

If the alpha particle has a stronger electric charge than an electron, why doesn't the alpha particle curve in its flight even more sharply than an electron does under the pull of a magnet? It has to be that the alpha particle is much heavier and more massive than the electron is. That would make it harder to pull the alpha particle out of a straight-line path. In fact, it turned out that an alpha particle is over 7,000 times as massive as an electron.

That means that an alpha particle is about four times as massive as an atom of hydrogen (HIGH-droh-jen), which is the lightest of all the atoms. In fact, an alpha particle is just about as massive as an atom of helium (HEE-lee-um).

Even though alpha particles were as massive as atoms, they had to be very tiny in size and much smaller than atoms. After all, alpha particles went through ordinary matter without trouble.

In 1906, Rutherford managed to trap quantities of alpha particles in a closed container. After a while, as more and more alpha particles entered the trap, Rutherford found he had helium present. There had been no helium in the trap before.

The alpha particles had somehow changed into helium. They weren't subatomic particles anymore; they were atoms. Yet their mass had not changed. Perhaps they had added electrons. Electrons have so little mass that their addition would hardly change the total mass of the atom.

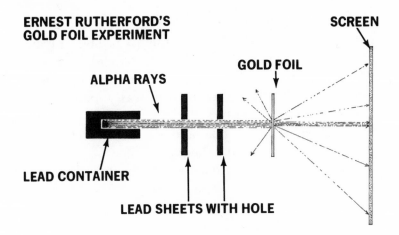

ERNEST RUTHERFORD'S GOLD FOIL EXPERIMENT

SCREEN

GOLD FOIL

ALPHA RAYS

LEAD CONTAINER

LEAD SHEETS WITH HOLE

Rutherford began another kind of experiment. He let flying alpha particles from radioactive substances hit a thin sheet of gold foil. The alpha particles almost always went through the foil without trouble. When they did, they hit a photographic plate on the other side of the foil and darkened it, and they hit exactly where they would have hit if the foil had not been there.

Every once in a while, though, an alpha particle would hit something in the gold foil and would bounce off. It would then darken a far corner of the photographic plate.

By 1909, Rutherford could say that most of the space in the atom was made up of a cloud of electrons. They were so light that a massive alpha particle just plowed right through them without trouble.

At the center of the atom, however, is a small but very massive "atomic nucleus" (NOO-klee-us); the plural of the word is "nuclei" (NOO-klee-igh). It is so small and takes up so little space that the alpha particles in Rutherford's experiments usually missed it. Every once in a while, though, an alpha particle would hit that very massive nucleus and would bounce off. The number of hits was so small that Rutherford could see that the nucleus had to be very tiny indeed. It would take about 100,000 nuclei, side by side, to stretch across the atom.

The alpha particle, then, was the bare nucleus of a helium atom. When an alpha particle picked up electrons here and there in its surroundings, it became an ordinary helium atom.

What makes different kinds of atoms different is the size of the electric charge on the nucleus, as was first shown in 1914 by the English scientist, Henry Gwyn-Jeffreys Moseley. For instance, the hydrogen nucleus has a charge of +1. Outside the hydrogen nucleus is one electron with a charge of − 1. The charges on the nucleus and on the electron balance each other, so that the whole atom has no charge.

In the same way, the helium nucleus has a charge of +2, and has two electrons outside, with a total charge of − 2 to balance it. The carbon nucleus has a charge of +6, with six electrons (− 6) to balance it. The oxygen nucleus has a charge of +8 with eight electrons (− 8) outside. The iron nucleus has a charge of +26 with 26 electrons (− 26) outside. And the uranium nucleus has a charge of +92, with 92 electrons (− 92) outside.

The size of the charge of the nucleus is called the "atomic number" of that element. Thus, hydrogen has an atomic number of 1, helium has an atomic

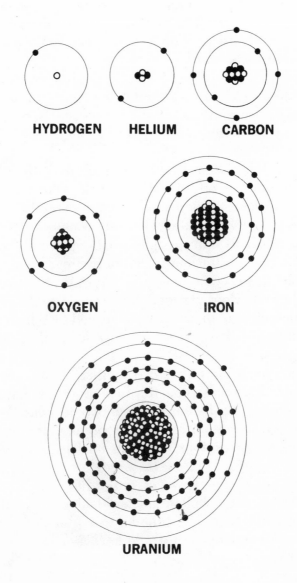

HYDROGEN **HELIUM** **CARBON**

OXYGEN **IRON**

URANIUM

23

number of 2, carbon has an atomic number of 6, oxygen has an atomic number of 8, iron has an atomic number of 26, uranium has an atomic number of 92, and so on. Scientists now know 105 different elements, with atomic numbers from 1 to 105. No atomic number is skipped.

By 1914, it seemed quite clear that every atom consisted of a tiny atomic nucleus surrounded by a cloud of electrons.

Since an atomic nucleus is so small, could it be a single particle?

That didn't seem likely. The nucleus of the uranium atom gives off an alpha particle, which is a helium nucleus. Other nuclei can give off smaller pieces, too. That made it possible to suppose that the atomic nucleus is made up of smaller particles.

The smallest nucleus is that of hydrogen and has a charge of +1, equal in size to that of the electron. In 1914, Rutherford decided that there couldn't be a smaller charge than that. He called the hydrogen nucleus a "proton" from a Greek word meaning "first."

It seemed likely that every other atomic nucleus contained protons, one for each positive charge it had. Thus, the helium nucleus would contain two protons; the carbon nucleus six protons; the oxygen nucleus eight protons; the iron nucleus 26 protons; and the uranium nucleus 92 protons.

This suggestion, however, didn't fit all the facts.

For instance, a helium nucleus had a charge of +2 and should therefore contain two protons. If that were all it contained, it would have a mass twice that

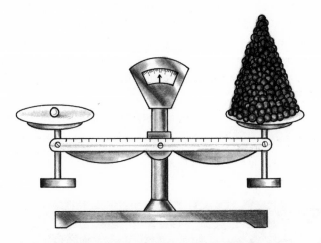

ONE PROTON BALANCES 1836 ELECTRONS.

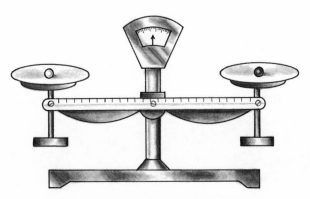

ONE NEUTRON BALANCES ONE PROTON

of a hydrogen nucleus, which is a single proton. However, the helium nucleus has a mass that can be measured and this turns out to be *four times* that of the hydrogen nucleus. That means that the two protons in the helium nucleus account for only half the mass. What accounts for the rest?

This difference between proton mass and atom mass is true for all the atoms with a charge greater than +1. The uranium nucleus contains 92 protons in

CLOUD CHAMBER TRACK OF A SLOW PROTON

CLOUD CHAMBER TRACK OF A FAST PROTON

SIR JAMES CHADWICK

its nucleus, for instance, but its mass is 238 times that of the hydrogen nucleus.

Scientists tried to figure out ways of accounting for that extra mass, but none of the solutions they tried really worked. Then, in 1932, an English scientist, James Chadwick, found the answer.

Scientists had developed ways of detecting streams of protons and electrons. The electric charges on those particles caused tiny water droplets to form around them, and a trail of droplets in special devices called "cloud chambers" marked the path of those particles.

When alpha particles struck the nuclei of an element named beryllium (beh-RIL-ee-um), however, a radiation was produced that didn't form any droplets. Scientists couldn't detect the radiation but they knew it was there because when it struck paraffin, it knocked protons out of the various nuclei in the paraffin.

Chadwick felt that *something* had to be knocking out those protons. Since a proton is a massive particle, what was knocking them out had to be massive, too. Electrons, for instance, were too light to knock protons out of a nucleus.

The massive new particle, whatever it was, couldn't have an electric charge or it would form water droplets and leave a trail. Chadwick said, therefore, that the radiation was made up of particles with about the size of a proton, but with no electric charge at all. The new particles were neither positively charged nor negatively charged. They were neutral, so he called the particle a "neutron" (NOO-tron).

That solved the problem of the atomic nuclei. They contained both protons and neutrons. The helium nucleus was made up of two protons and two neutrons. The two protons gave it its charge of +2. The two protons and two neutrons, altogether, gave it a mass four times that of the hydrogen nuclei's single proton.

The same was true of other nuclei. Except for hydrogen with its single-proton nucleus, all contained both protons and neutrons. The uranium nucleus contains 92 protons and 146 neutrons. Its charge is +92, but its mass is 92 +146, or 238 times that of the proton.

Every atomic nucleus of a particular element has the same number of protons. The number of neutrons, however, may differ slightly from atom to atom. For instance, some uranium nuclei contain 92 protons, but only 143 neutrons. The charge is still +92, but the mass is 92 + 143, or 235 times that of the proton.

Nuclei with the same number of protons but with different numbers of neutrons are called "isotopes" (EYE-soh-topes). These are named according to the total number of particles in the nuclei. The uranium nucleus with 92 protons and 146 neutrons is "uranium-238." The one with 92 protons and 143 neutrons is "uranium-235."

Isotopes of a particular element aren't equally common. One might be very common, and one might be rare. For instance, out of every 1,000 uranium atoms, 993 are uranium-238, and only seven are uranium-235.

PIERRE CURIE

3

Nuclear Energy

THE RADIATIONS produced by a radioactive element such as uranium have a great deal of energy. Gamma rays have much more energy than light, for instance. The alpha and beta particles move at speeds of tens of thousands of miles per second and that makes them very energetic, too.

The first to try to determine just how much energy is produced by radioactive elements was French scientist Pierre Curie, the husband of Marie Curie. In 1901, he measured the amount of energy given off by a radioactive element called "radium" (RAY-dee-um), which he and his wife had discovered three years before.

Only tiny amounts of radium existed, but his measurements showed that if an ounce of it could be put together in one spot, the energy of the particles and rays it would give off in one hour would be about 4,000 calories.

In one way, this isn't much. When an ounce of gasoline is burned, it produces 325,000 calories, or about 80 times as much energy in one hour as radium.

Once you've burned the ounce of gasoline, however, that's all the energy you're going to get out of it. There isn't any more. The radium, on the other hand, keeps right on going after it has produced 4,000 calories of energy in one hour.

In another hour, the ounce of radium produces another 4,000 calories, and in another hour another 4,000 calories, and so on. After 80 hours, it has produced as much energy as you can get by burning the gasoline. After 800 hours it has produced 10 times as much energy as you can get by burning the gasoline. After 8,000 hours, it has produced 100 times as much energy, and so on.

To be sure, the rate at which radium produces energy does get less with time, but only very slowly. Eventually, the rate of energy production drops to only half of what it was originally, but that is only after radium has been giving off energy for 1,620 years. By the time the radium stops radiating altogether, it will have produced about a quarter of a million times as much energy as the same weight of burning gasoline.

Where does all that energy come from?

Since the 1840's, scientists have been quite certain that energy has to come from somewhere° and that goes for the energy of radioactivity, too.

° See HOW DID WE FIND OUT ABOUT ENERGY? (Walker, 1975)

Scientists were well acquainted with the energy produced when chemicals combined with each other. When wood or coal or gasoline burns, for instance, carbon and hydrogen atoms in the fuel combine with oxygen atoms in the air and that produces energy. This kind of combination is called a "chemical reaction" and the energy produced in this way is "chemical energy."

Once scientists understood how atoms were constructed, they could see that chemical reactions took place when electrons shifted from one atom to another. Some electron arrangements contain a great deal of energy tied up in the atomic structure; others contain less. When the arrangements shift from high energy content to low energy content, what happens to the extra energy? It is given off as light, as heat, and as other forms of energy.

But that was just the electrons. What about the protons and neutrons in the atomic nuclei? Some proton-neutron arrangements contain a great deal of energy tied up in the structure. Other arrangements contain less. If a high-energy arrangement shifts to a low-energy arrangement, again the extra energy is given off. This time it is given off in the form of very short-wave radiation or very high-speed particles.

In radioactivity, the protons and neutrons in the nuclei of uranium, thorium, radium and other such elements, are rearranged in a way so as to tie up less energy. This is called a "nuclear reaction." The excess energy is liberated, and this is called "nuclear energy." (Sometimes it is called "atomic energy.")

The protons and neutrons of the nucleus are far

more massive than electrons. They are held more closely and more tightly together than electrons. This means that the amount of energy tied up in proton-neutron structure is much higher than the amount tied up in electron structure. That is why the energy released is so much greater in the case of radioactivity than in the case of burning gasoline.

When scientists studied the different nuclei, they came to realize that those of middle size had the least energy. Very massive nuclei like those of uranium and thorium contain much energy. If they rearrange themselves into somewhat smaller nuclei with less energy, then the extra energy they had to start with is given off as radiation and particles.

In the same way, the lightest nuclei would tie up less energy if their particles were rearranged into somewhat larger nuclei. Again, the extra energy would be given off as radiation and particles.

This furnished the answer to a question that had puzzled scientists for nearly a hundred years. The sun gives off very large quantities of energy in every direction and has been doing it for many hundreds of millions of years. Where does that energy come from? There was no really satisfying answer to that question at first.

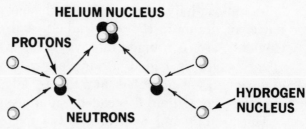

HYDROGEN FUSING TO FORM HELIUM

Astronomers had, however, found out that the sun was mostly hydrogen. A German-American scientist, Hans Albrecht Bethe (BAY-tuh), showed in 1938 that four hydrogen nuclei, each made up of one proton, could rearrange themselves into one helium nucleus made up of two protons and two neutrons. As a result, energy would be released. That would account for the sun's ability to shine for so long a time. It was thanks to nuclear energy.

Of course, once scientists understood nuclear energy, and what an enormous supply of it there was locked in atomic nuclei, they began to wonder if people could make use of it to do the work of the world. People had been using the chemical energy of shifting electrons when they burned wood, coal, or oil, and had been doing so for many thousands of years. Could they now begin to use the nuclear energy of shifting protons and neutrons as well?

When energy is used by human beings to do work, it is called "power." The question was, then, whether mankind could take advantage of "nuclear power."

Yet though there is a lot of nuclear energy, it comes out slowly. The most common radioactive elements are uranium and thorium and their energy takes *billions of years* to come out.

What's more, it isn't easy for scientists to make that energy come out faster. In dealing with chemical reactions, it is easy to speed it up. A match doesn't seem to be burning before it is lit, but the chemicals of the match are slowly combining with oxygen in the air. However, once we heat the match

HANS A. BETHE

by rubbing it against a rough surface the rate of combination speeds up and the match bursts into flame. A jar of nitroglycerine just sits there, but strike it with something and it will explode.

That is because electrons are in the outer parts of atoms. They are easily reached by heat and by blows or other changes that can speed the rate at which they transfer from atom to atom.

The nuclei, on the other hand, are hidden deep within the center of atoms. They can't be reached easily. For instance, you can't speed up the radioactivity of uranium by heating it, or hitting it, or doing anything else that would speed up a chemical reaction. The uranium just keeps on delivering its energy very, very slowly—too slowly to be useful as a source of power.

What is needed is something that will manage to go right through the outer part of the atom, with all its electrons, and strike right at the nucleus itself.

The only things that scientists knew of, at first, to do the job, were subatomic particles. The most efficient ones were the alpha particles that are sent out by various radioactive elements. These are so massive that they can just plow through electrons as though they weren't there.

What would happen if an alpha particle hit a nucleus?

NUCLEAR CHANGE OF NITROGEN INTO OXYGEN

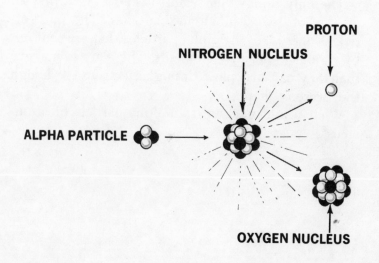

PROTON

NITROGEN NUCLEUS

ALPHA PARTICLE

OXYGEN NUCLEUS

4 Nuclear Reactions

THE FIRST ONE TO TRY purposefully to strike nuclei with alpha particles was Rutherford. In 1919, he sent alpha particles crashing into a container of a gas called nitrogen (NIGHT-roh-jen). Every once in a while, he could detect speeding protons in the container. Where did they come from?

What happened was that the alpha particle would, every once in a while, hit a nitrogen nucleus and send a proton flying out of it. The alpha particle would stick to what was left of the nitrogen nucleus. The nitrogen nucleus started with seven protons. It lost one, but it gained the two of the alpha particle. It ended with eight protons and that made it an oxygen nucleus.

This was the first *human-made* nuclear reaction. It was the first time that anyone had changed one element into another.

ERNEST RUTHERFORD

Rutherford also produced nuclear reactions when he bombarded other elements with alpha particles.

The alpha particles produced by radioactive substances only have a certain amount of energy, however. They can only strike nuclei with a certain amount of force and can produce only a few nuclear reactions.

Scientists tried to work out ways of making subatomic particles move faster and faster and strike with more and more energy.

When the scientists heated hydrogen, they could knock off the single electron in each atom and leave behind the bare nucleus consisting of a single proton. The proton could then be brought under the influence of a magnet. A properly arranged device could make the magnet pull the proton along and make it go faster and faster. Finally, when the proton had gained an enormous amount of energy, it could speed out of the device and smash into a nucleus, rearranging the protons and neutrons within it.

The first people to build such an "atom-smasher" were an English scientist, John Douglas Cockcroft, and his Irish partner, Ernest Thomas Sinton Walton. They built the device in 1929. In 1931, they used fast protons to break up the atomic nucleus of the light element lithium (LITH-ee-um).

Other scientists built other kinds of atom-smashers. The most successful atom-smasher was one built by the American scientist, Ernest Orlando Lawrence. In 1930, he built the first "cyclotron" (SIGH-kloh-tron).

The cyclotron was so constructed as to make the magnet drive the protons round and round in a slowly expanding circle. The protons moved faster and

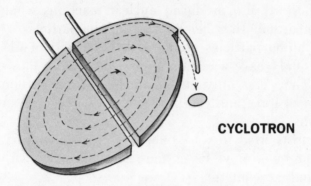

CYCLOTRON

faster as they went around and by the time their circular movement expanded to the point where they came pouring out of the cyclotron, they had enormous energies.

All through the 1930's, scientists kept bombarding all kinds of nuclei with more and more energetic protons. They produced more and more nuclear reactions. They kept rearranging protons and neutrons and learned a great deal about how atomic nuclei were built up.

Although scientists learned more and more about nuclei, they weren't learning how to make use of nuclear power. The nuclear reactions they brought about did produce a little energy, but only very little. What's more, scientists had to use up a great deal of energy to produce those speeding protons. Very few of the protons actually hit nuclei. Most of them just sped along and hit nothing, and their energy was wasted.

The result was that atom-smashing scientists used enormous quantities of electrical and magnetic energy to produce just a little bit of nuclear energy.

When Rutherford died, in 1937, he was still sure that people would never learn how to use nuclear power. He thought they would always have to put in more energy than they got out.

One trouble with using alpha particles and protons is that they carry positive electric charges. Atomic nuclei also carry positive electric charges. Two positive charges repel each other; that is, they push each other away. Whenever an alpha particle or a proton approaches a nucleus, it veers away a bit because of the repulsion. For that reason, the number of hits is reduced.

What about the neutron, though? It has no electric charge at all, and nuclei would not repel it. Still, could a neutron have enough energy to bring about a nuclear reaction?

Protons are made to move faster and to gain energy by a magnet pulling at its electric charge. Since a neutron has no charge, it can't be pulled and made to move faster.

In 1934, an Italian scientist, Enrico Fermi (FEHR-mee), decided that it wasn't necessary to make neutrons move fast. Suppose neutrons just crept along slowly and had very little energy. If they just happened to be moving in the right direction, one of them might come up to an atomic nucleus and melt into it. The nucleus's positive charge wouldn't push the neutron away.

That added neutron might upset the proton-neutron arrangement of the nucleus and cause it to begin rearranging itself.

ENRICO FERMI

Fermi began to bombard nuclei with slow neutrons and found that in many cases a nucleus absorbed the neutron, then rearranged itself in such a way as to change the neutron into a proton. The nucleus would then end up with one more proton than it had to begin with. It became a new element that was one higher in atomic number than the old one.

For instance, Fermi bombarded nuclei of the element rhodium (ROH-dee-um), which has an atomic number of 45, and ended with palladium (puh-LAY-dee-um), which has an atomic number of 46. As another example, he turned indium (IN-dee-um), with an atomic number of 49, into tin, with an atomic number of 50.

At that time, the element with the highest known atomic number was uranium, which had an atomic number of 92. Was it possible, Fermi wondered, to bombard uranium with neutrons and produce a new element with atomic number 93? Element 93 wasn't known in nature, and Fermi would in that way form a brand-new element.

Fermi bombarded uranium with slow neutrons and then he tried to check the kinds of radiation that resulted. From the different radiations and from the amount of energy each had, scientists could often decide what new kinds of nuclei had been formed.

Fermi thought he might have formed the new element 93, but the radiation results were confusing and he wasn't sure.

Others tackled the problem, too. One of them was a German scientist, Otto Hahn, who worked with an

Austrian partner, Lise Meitner (MIGHT-ner).

They wondered if, perhaps, the uranium atom might not be gaining particles, but might rather be losing them. Suppose the atom gave off a pair of alpha particles. If two alpha particles (with four protons altogether) split away from uranium's 92, what would be left would be radium with an atomic number of 88.

Any radium would be present only in very tiny quantities. How could its presence be detected?

One way was to make use of an element named barium (BA-ree-um). Barium has an atomic number of 56, but it has chemical properties that are very similar to those of radium. Anything that happens to barium will also happen to radium.

What Hahn and Meitner did, in 1938, was to add barium to uranium and then take it out again. Whatever they did to take out the barium would also take out the radium. That meant it would take out the radiation that Hahn and Meitner thought might be caused by radium.

Sure enough, when the barium came out, the radiation came out with it. Hahn and Meitner felt sure that their theory was correct and that radium had been formed from the uranium.

Next they tried to separate the radiation by using chemical methods that would separate radium from barium. They failed. Whatever they did, the radiation stayed with the barium.

Then something happened to upset their work. Adolf Hitler was ruling Germany at that time and he was driving Jewish people out of their jobs and otherwise persecuting them. Lise Meitner was Jewish but she was also Austrian and was therefore safe for a while. In March 1938, however, Hitler sent his troops into Austria and took that country over. Meitner was no longer safe. She got out of the country and went to Sweden.

In Sweden, she thought about the problem she had been working on with Hahn, and wondered if there was any radium in their barium after all. Perhaps the barium was nothing but barium. Perhaps when neutrons bombarded uranium, a special radioactive kind of barium was formed. This new barium came out of the uranium with the ordinary barium which had been added to the uranium and then, of course, the two could not be separated.

But how could barium, with an atomic number of 56, be made from uranium with an atomic number of 92?

The biggest particle that had been known to split away from a nucleus was an alpha particle, and that had an atomic number of 2. Eighteen alpha particles would have to split away from a single uranium nucleus to form barium, and there was no sign that this had happened.

Meitner wondered if, perhaps, barium was formed all in one step. Suppose the neutron made the uranium nucleus split in two, forming smaller nuclei, including barium as well as others. Such a split is sometimes called "fission" (FISH-un), so Meitner was thinking about "uranium fission."

Along with her nephew, Otto Robert Frisch, Meitner wrote an announcement suggesting her

NILS BOHR

ideas about uranium fission. It was printed in January 1939. Before it was printed, Frisch discussed the notion with a Danish scientist, Niels Bohr.

Bohr was on his way to the United States at the time to attend a meeting of scientists interested in atomic nuclei and nuclear reactions. He told them the idea and they all left the meeting immediately to test the idea in their laboratories.

Once they studied what happened when neutrons struck uranium, with the possibility of fission in their minds, they could see that it must be exactly what happened.

When neutrons hit uranium nuclei, those nuclei split into two parts—and produced a particularly large amount of energy.

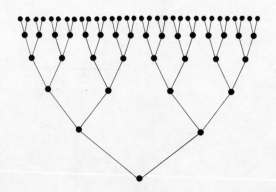

CHAIN REACTION

5 Nuclear Reactors

ONE PERSON WHO HEARD the news about uranium fission was the Hungarian scientist, Leo Szilard (ZEE-lahrd). He noticed that when a uranium atom fissioned, it produced two or three neutrons.

Suppose a uranium atom split and produced two neutrons and each of the two neutrons struck a uranium atom. Two uranium atoms would split and produce four neutrons altogether. They would split four uranium atoms and produce eight neutrons, and so on.

Each fissioning uranium atom would split others in greater and greater numbers. Each nuclear reaction would link to others and form a chain. It would be a "chain reaction."

That happened with chemical energy when you lit

the corner of a large piece of paper with a match. The heat of the burning paper would start nearby parts burning until finally the whole sheet would be afire. The heat given off by the entire sheet would be far greater than the original heat of the match.

In the same way, each splitting uranium atom would produce a little energy. This energy would mount up as more and more uranium atoms split. Far more energy would be produced by the fission than was put in by the original neutron.

Of course, fissioning uranium atoms involved nuclear energy. The nuclear chain reaction was much, *much* faster than the chemical chain reaction that made paper burn. The energy produced by the fissioning uranium atoms would be much, *much* greater than the energy produced by burning paper.

Uranium fission made it seem that people would finally be able to use nuclear power. At last they would get out more than they put in, something Rutherford had suspected would never be possible.

But fission power might be dangerous. It seemed to Szilard that if a quantity of uranium were made to undergo fission it would produce so much energy that it would explode. What's more, the explosion of only a little bit of uranium would be as great as that of thousands of tons of ordinary chemical explosives.

The thought made him nervous. Szilard had left Europe because of Hitler's persecutions, and he was sure that Hitler intended to start a war soon. What if German scientists worked out a "nuclear fission bomb"? (Such a bomb is also called an "atom bomb" or an "A-bomb.")

LEO SZILARD

If Hitler got his hands on such a weapon, he could use it to win a war. The whole world might then be under a cruel and unjust government.

Szilard, therefore, thought it was important for the United States to get the nuclear fission bomb first.

The most famous scientist in the world, at the time, was Albert Einstein. He, too, had fled Germany and was living in the United States. Szilard and others persuaded him to write a letter to the American president, Franklin Delano Roosevelt, explaining the situation. The letter was mailed on August 2, 1939; one month later, World War II started in Europe.

On December 6, 1941, President Roosevelt finally ordered a huge effort to develop a nuclear fission bomb. The very next day, Japan attacked Pearl Harbor and the United States found itself in World War II.

Many scientists from America and other countries began to collect uranium and to try to work out ways for setting off a chain reaction in it. Naturally, they wanted a chain reaction that would not go out of control. A metal called cadmium (KAD-mee-um) absorbs neutrons safely, so cadmium rods were placed in the uranium to keep too many neutrons from fissioning too many uranium atoms.

It was found that it wasn't uranium-238 that was split by neutrons, but the rare isotope, uranium-235. Ways were developed to separate the two isotopes and prepare uranium that was richer in uranium-235.

Meanwhile, new elements were formed with very massive nuclei of the kind Fermi had tried to form

J. ROBERT OPPENHEIMER

some years before. Element 93 was named "neptunium" (nep-TOO-nee-um) and element 94 was named "plutonium" (ploo-TOH-nee-um). It turned out that plutonium could be made to undergo fission, too.

Fermi had left Italy now and, in the United States, he headed the group of scientists trying to get the nuclear fission chain reaction going. On December 2, 1942, they succeeded. In Chicago, the first "nuclear reactor" began to yield energy by way of a nuclear fission chain reaction that was kept under control.

A team of scientists, under the leadership of J. Robert Oppenheimer, spent the next few years trying to collect enough uranium-235 and plutonium to make nuclear fission bombs. On July 16, 1945, the first nuclear fission bomb exploded at Alamogordo, New Mexico. The explosion was tremendous.

Two more bombs were prepared. By then, Germany had surrendered, but Japan was still fighting. One of the bombs was exploded over the Japanese city of Hiroshima on August 6, 1945, and the other over Nagasaki, two days later. The Japanese government surrendered, and World War II came to an end.

Of course, nuclear fission didn't have to be used just in bombs. If the fission were controlled, energy could be used without explosions. Scientists tried to make additional nuclear reactors that were smaller, more efficient, and more useful than the first one made in Chicago.

In 1954, a new submarine, the USS Nautilus, was launched. It carried on board a nuclear reactor which provided all its power. Ordinary submarines have to come to the surface frequently to charge their batteries, but nuclear submarines can stay underwater for months at a time.

Nuclear reactors were being built for peacetime use, also. The Soviet Union built a small one in 1954, then the British built a larger one. Finally, in 1958, the United States completed a still larger one at Shippingport, Pennsylvania.

When nuclear power first began to be used in the 1950's, it was hoped that this would be a vast new source of energy for the people of the world. There turned out to be problems, though.

There wasn't really much uranium-235 in the world. Would nuclear power come to an end when the uranium-235 was used up?

U S S NAUTILUS

NUCLEAR REACTOR AT SAN CLEMENTE, CALIFORNIA

But then scientists learned it was possible to surround a nuclear reactor with ordinary uranium or with thorium. Some of the neutrons from the nuclear reactor brought about changes in the uranium or thorium that turned them into nuclei that could be fissioned. In this way more fuel could be formed than was used up in the reactor. Such a "breeder reactor" could make use of all the uranium and thorium, not just uranium-235. With breeder reactors, human beings could count on nuclear power for hundreds of thousands of years.

However, there was danger. Breeder reactors use plutonium which is about the most dangerous material in the world. It produces radioactive compounds that can be very dangerous and stay dangerous for thousands of years. There might not be any really good ways to dispose of these compounds, and accidents at the reactor might spread them over hundreds of square miles.

By the 1970's, more and more people were wondering whether nuclear fission power is safe enough to be used. Perhaps other kinds of power should be used instead.

There *is* another kind of nuclear power. Why not work at the other end of the list of elements? Why not start with hydrogen nuclei and form helium nuclei out of them as the sun does?

The process of combining several small nuclei into one larger nucleus is called "nuclear fusion" (FYOO-zhun). Nuclear fusion produces much more energy than nuclear fission for a given weight of fuel. What's more, hydrogen, which is the fuel for fusion, is far more common than the various elements that are the fuel for fission. Also, fusion produces less radioactivity than fission does, so fusion is safer.

Getting hydrogen nuclei to fuse isn't easy though. It takes temperatures of hundreds of millions of degrees to make fusion take place.

One way of getting such tremendously high temperatures is to use a fission bomb. If a fission bomb is set off in such a way as to make a mass of hydrogen begin to fuse, an explosion takes place that is enormously larger than one caused by the fission bomb alone.

This much larger bomb is called a "hydrogen bomb," or an "H-bomb." It can also be called a "nuclear fusion bomb."

The first nuclear fusion bomb was exploded by the United States in 1952 over the Marshall Islands in the Pacific Ocean. Eventually, nuclear fusion bombs were constructed that were thousands of times as powerful as the first nuclear fission bombs of 1945. Fortunately, nuclear fusion bombs have never so far been used in war.

But can there be *controlled* nuclear fusion? Can hydrogen be heated up to hundreds of millions of degrees and made to fuse in very small quantities? Can it be made to give off energy *without* exploding?

Scientists in the United States and in other countries have been trying to bring this about for thirty years now and they haven't yet succeeded. Still, they are making progress.

To bring about fusion, they are making use of a

special variety of hydrogen called "deuterium" (doo-TEE-ree-um). The deuterium nucleus contains one proton and one neutron, instead of just a proton as ordinary hudrogen atoms do.

Deuterium nuclei have been heated to very high temperatures and have then been held in place with powerful magnetic devices. So far, though, scientists have not managed to make the deuterium quite hot enough, or hold it in place quite long enough, for fusion to begin.

Eventually, scientists may do this. Once that happens, there will be a very large source of nuclear power ready for use. It should be safe to use—much safer than fission, anyway—and it could last us for many millions of years.

We have come far in a single century. A hundred years ago, scientists were wondering what cathode rays might be. Now they are trying to make a miniature sun on the earth, a little sun that will do the work of the world.

Index